SHEFFIELD PARK GARDEN

East Sussex

The National Trust

Introduction

The great ponds at Sheffield Place at the right season of the year are bordered with red, white and purple reflections, for rhododendrons are massed upon the banks and when the wind passes over the real flowers the water flowers shake and break into each other.

Virginia Woolf, 'Reflections on Sheffield Place', 1937

The combination of water and flowers has always attracted gardeners, and at Sheffield Park Garden (as it is now known) the two are brought together with superb effect.

The series of four great lakes, around which the garden is laid out, began at the bottom of the gently sloping valley and was gradually extended north-west up towards the house during the eighteenth century by the 1st Earl of Sheffield, with the advice of 'Capability' Brown and Humphry Repton. In the nineteenth century the 3rd Earl made Sheffield Park famous for country-house cricket, and also transformed the garden into an arboretum of exotic and native conifers. But it was not until 1910 and the arrival of Arthur Gilstrap Soames that the garden really began to blossom. He planted the clumps of lakeside rhododendrons enjoyed by Virginia Woolf, and provided spectacular autumn colour with Japanese maples, nyssas and beds of autumn gentians. Indeed today, with the summer-flowering water-lilies, there is colour to be enjoyed around Sheffield Park's lakes throughout the visitor season. And the descendants of the swans that the young Maria Josepha Holroyd watched from her window over 200 years ago still glide across these tranquil waters.

Anne North standing by the First Lake in 1798, the year she married the future 1st Earl of Sheffield, who laid out the framework of the garden we see today; drawing by Henry Edridge (National Portrait Gallery)

Reflections in the First Lake

Early History

Sheffield Park Garden may be a relatively recent creation, but this landscape has had a long history of human involvement. The name 'Sheffield' appears in the Domesday Book, when it meant 'sheep clearing', which suggests that this well-wooded part of Sussex south of Ashdown Forest had been open country since Saxon times. Water has also always played an important part in the landscape: the lower stretches of the valley, south of where the Woman's Way Ponds now are, were often flooded by the River Ouse. Domesday mentions a watermill at Sheffield and that local tenants paid their rent in eels.

By the mid-fifteenth century the sheep pasture had become a deer-park. In the following century the deer seem to have gone, as the burgeoning Wealden iron industry stimulated more efficient harvesting of coppiced timber for charcoal, and the park increasingly reverted to pasture.

The first detailed visual record of the area that has survived is the estate map drawn up in 1745 for John, 1st Earl de la Warr, whose family was one of the oldest established in the area and had owned Sheffield Place intermittently since 1292. The estate had several other owners of national significance: Robert, Count of Mortain, the half-brother of William the Conqueror; Simon de Montfort, who camped his rebel army nearby before his victory over Henry III at the Battle of Lewes in 1264; in the 1380s, Sir Edward Dalyngrigge, the builder of Bodiam Castle; and Thomas Howard, 3rd Duke of Norfolk, who entertained Henry VIII here in August 1538. It also belonged to two other famous local families, the Sackvilles and, from 1623, the Nevilles, but none of them used it as their primary residence, and perhaps as a result we know very little about what these early owners did to the estate.

The 1745 map reveals that Lord de la Warr had been landscaping the former deer-park since at least 1730 with a formal design of the kind popular at that time. He planted long avenues of oak and ash running northwards from the house (which was on the site of the present mansion), and rows of chestnut, walnut and cherry trees running east. Between 1745 and 1769 he created a lake from what had been no more than a stream, on the site of the present Upper and Lower Woman's Way Ponds. The inventory taken on his death in 1766 lists seven garden seats 'in the Wood and upon the lawn', including a stuccoed 'Gothick Seat', from which strollers could doubtless enjoy the views across the formal garden and lake.

A seventeenth-century fireback from nearby Bateman's, showing a Wealden ironmaster with the tools of his trade. From the sixteenth century the surrounding woodland was heavily coppiced to provide charcoal for this important local industry

Thomas Howard, 3rd Duke of Norfolk, who entertained Henry VIII at Sheffield Place in August 1538, around the time this portrait by Holbein was painted (Royal Collection)

John Baker Holroyd, 1st Earl of Sheffield (1735–1821)

In 1769 the 2nd Earl de la Warr, burdened by money problems, sold the Sheffield estate for £30,000 to John Baker Holroyd, who was created Baron Sheffield in 1781 and Earl of Sheffield in 1816. Lord Sheffield is best remembered today for his close friendship with the great historian Edward Gibbon, who was a frequent visitor to Sheffield Park; here Gibbon always felt, as he put it, 'safe, happy and at home'. Several chapters of his masterpiece, *The Decline and Fall of the Roman Empire*, were written in the Sheffield Park library. Whether he cared much for the park is doubtful: as Sheffield's daughter, Maria Josepha, noted, 'Gib is a mortal enemy to any person taking a walk.' Gibbon chose Lord Sheffield as his literary executor, and after he died in London in 1794, his body was brought down to Sheffield Park to be buried, under a crimson cloth, in the Sheffield family mausoleum in nearby Fletching church.

John Baker Holroyd, 1st Earl of Sheffield; drawing by Henry Edridge, 1798 (National Portrait Gallery)

The historian Edward Gibbon, who was a close friend of Lord Sheffield and a frequent visitor to Sheffield Place; painting by Henry Walton, *c.* 1773 (National Portrait Gallery)

Bernard Scale's ornate map of 1774 shows the park in the early years of its transformation by the 1st Earl of Sheffield. At the bottom is a long tree-lined lake, where the Woman's Way Ponds are today (East Sussex County Record Office)

Lord Sheffield was also an active politician, particularly in the fields of trade and finance, and, like most politicians, had a higher opinion of his own abilities than did his contemporaries. He had more success and influence as an agricultural 'improver', serving as President of the Board of Agriculture and transforming the run-down Sheffield estate by establishing a model home farm on his property. He also called in one of the most fashionable architects of the day, James Wyatt, who remodelled the house in the Gothick style c.1776–7, and again c.1780–90, and added an elegant crenellated lodge.

At the same time Lord Sheffield set about transforming the already extensive pleasure grounds around the house. In 1774–5 he had Gibbon track down the equally busy and fashionable 'Capability' Brown, who sent over one of his assistants, a Mr Spyers, the following year. Frustratingly little evidence survives of what Brown actually did at Sheffield Park. He seems to have concentrated not primarily on new planting, but on clearing informal paths through Sheffield Wood to the east of the house, and on creating pleasingly irregular belts, clumps and groves of trees in the park by careful felling. Samuel Grimm's 1787 view of the 'Great Water' shows what is now the First Lake, or Ten-Foot Pond, to have been at this time long, tree-lined and surrounded by open expanses of grass in typically Brownian fashion.

'Capability' Brown, who worked at Sheffield Place in the mid-1770s; painting by Nathaniel Dance, c.1770? (National Portrait Gallery)

'The Great Water'; watercolour by Samuel Hieronymus Grimm, 1787 (British Library). Grimm's view looks east from the house across the tree-lined First Lake towards the spire of Fletching church, in which Gibbon is buried

Humphry Repton at Sheffield Park

'Capability' Brown's most influential immediate successor, Humphry Repton, also worked at Sheffield Park as one of his earliest assignments. Alas, no Red Book survives, if one was ever made, and again it is difficult to be certain about his precise contribution. He visited several times in 1789 and 1790, and seems to have concentrated his efforts near the house where he created a series of four small lakes on the site of the present-day First Lake. Repton himself mentions 'A very beautiful lake has been added to the scenery of a place which abounds in the most perfect specimens of the picturesque effects produced by Gothic architecture.' He also appears to have increased the planting beside the lakes and to have divided the lower lake into two with a bridge.

However, Repton seems to have fallen out with Lord Sheffield. Certainly, not all his plans were carried out and he lamented, 'Such is the power of vegetation at Sheffield Place, that every berry soon becomes a bush, and every bush a tree.' As a result, 'the natural shape of the vale is obliterated, the gently sloping banks are covered with wood, and the narrow glade in the bottom is choked with spreading larches.' Lord Sheffield himself was delighted that his trees were so vigorous, and, looking back in 1813, only wished he had appreciated earlier the commercial potential of woodland, especially when carefully pruned: 'Certainly the growth of timber should be the greatest object in the neighbourhood, where it grows so remarkably well.'

By the 1790s the park had expanded north, south and east with new plantations, principally of oak and ash, surrounded by pasture; 500 sycamores were planted in 1793 alone. Although Lord Sheffield was often away on parliamentary business, his family made full use of the garden. A favourite spot was Sylph Place, a wooded peninsula at the south-west end of the Third Lake, or Upper Woman's Way Pond. (The pond takes its name from the ghost of a headless woman, which is said, according to local legend, to wander this part of the garden.) Nearby was an ornamental gun battery, from which a salute was fired over the lake in 1809 to celebrate the Golden Jubilee of George III's accession.

Under George Holroyd, the 2nd Earl, who succeeded his father in 1821, the park seems to have been somewhat neglected, perhaps for lack of money. According to one observer, it was 'over-crowded with massive timber which had stood for generations'.

Humphry Repton, who remodelled the garden as a young man

Repton recommended 'the picturesque effect which is always produced by the mixture of Gothic buildings with *round-headed* trees'

An eighteenth-century watercolour of Sheffield Place, which was remodelled in the Gothick style by James Wyatt for the 1st Lord Sheffield

CRICKET MATCH

BETWEEN THE

Australian Eleven

AND THE

Earl of Sheffield's Eleven

Sheffield Park

May 12th., 1896

Henry Holroyd, 3rd Earl of Sheffield (1832–1909)

Henry Holroyd, the future 3rd Earl, joined the diplomatic service and was MP for East Sussex from 1857 to 1865, but his real love was cricket. As an eager thirteen-year-old, he took part in the first recorded cricket match at Sheffield Park, in August 1845. He was later good enough to play for the Gentlemen of Sussex. So when he inherited Sheffield Park in 1876, one of his first priorities was to build a cricket pitch on the estate, which he did by levelling the area to the south-east of the Upper Woman's Way Pond. The project also had the added advantage of providing much-needed winter employment at a time of agricultural depression. In 1882–3 he put up an octagonal pavilion, adorned with climbing shrubs and its own garden; a separate pavilion for the ladies was added later.

Sheffield Park has an important place in the early history of England–Australia cricket. Between 1884 and 1896 the Australian team opened their tour with a match against Lord Sheffield's XI. The final match was attended by the Prince of Wales and watched by over 25,000 spectators, all admitted free. On that occasion Lord Sheffield's team included W. G. Grace as captain (he made 49 in the first innings), Prince Ranjitsinhji, C. B. Fry and F. S. Jackson. On the evening of the second day the teams sat down to a gargantuan dinner which included a choice of ten different main courses. Perhaps not surprisingly, the match was drawn. Lord Sheffield also helped to get Australian state cricket started by presenting the Sheffield Shield trophy as a prize.

The Sheffield Shield, the trophy given by Lord Sheffield for the Australian State cricket competition (Australian Gallery of Sport and Olympic Museum, Melbourne)

Lord Sheffield's XI, standing in front of his elegant cricket pavilion in 1886. W. G. Grace, the team captain, is seated in the centre

A menu card for the dinner held during the match between the Australian touring team and Lord Sheffield's XI in May 1896 (Lord's Cricket Museum)

The Top Bridge, built for the 3rd Earl between the First and Second Lakes in 1882–5

Ghent azaleas

The 3rd Earl did much to revive the rest of the Sheffield Park garden. He drained the Ten-Foot Pond in order to enlarge it, and created the present Second, or Middle, Lake from two of Repton's rectangular ponds below. At the top and bottom of the new Middle Lake, he commissioned artificial waterfalls from Pulham & Son, a firm which had been famous since the 1840s for its decorative garden rockwork made from 'Pulhamite' – Portland cement over a rubble core, modelled to resemble natural stone. However, as good sandstone was freely available locally, there was no need to resort to Pulhamite in this case. The firm also supplied the stonework for the Top Bridge, between 1882 and 1885; indeed they later marketed the design as the 'Uckfield Balustrade'. The 'Grand Cascade', between the Upper and Lower Woman's Way Ponds, was constructed around the same date, but not by Pulham.

With the aid of his gardener, William Thomas Moore, the 3rd Earl laid out the basic skeleton of the planting we see today. The view south-east from the house down over a series of 'water terraces' to the cricket pitch became the principal axis, around which the major planting was conceived. By 1885 he had begun an arboretum, planted mostly north of the lakes and consisting of exotic and native trees, including conifers (Scotch pines, wellingtonia and maritime pines along the lakeside walks), rhododendrons, azaleas and Japanese acers. By the falls there were Silver Deodars, Golden Retinospora, Golden-leaved Weigela and British ferns. He is said to have brought back rare varieties from his diplomatic posting in Constantinople, but it has so far been impossible to identify these. He was certainly keen on providing spring colour in the garden, to coincide with the opening of the cricket season and the Australian tour matches, which usually took place in May.

The 3rd Earl's later years were clouded by disputes with his neighbours, threatening letters and increasing money worries. He never married and spent long periods in France, where he died in April 1909, leaving no heir and an estate heavily in debt.

The 'Grand Cascade' created in the 1880s

The Soames Era (1910–53)

One of the 3rd Earl's principal creditors was Arthur Gilstrap Soames, a wealthy Lincolnshire brewer who had fallen in love with the garden while staying nearby in 1889. He had asked Lord Sheffield for the first option to purchase the estate after his death, and did so, from his executors, in 1910.

Soames seems to have begun planting on an ambitious scale almost immediately, bringing in thousands of cartloads of loam to improve the soil. His great loves were roses and rhododendrons. Yellow Banksian roses were trained round the drawing-room windows. He planted the rhododendrons for which Sheffield Park is now famous in carefully arranged clumps, principally along the north side of the Ten-Foot Pond and Middle Lake for spring colour. Among a fine collection of hardy hybrid rhododendrons is *R.* 'Angelo', which was bred at Sheffield Park by Mr Soames, and the late-flowering *R.* 'Loderi'. For autumn colour – perhaps Sheffield Park's greatest attraction – Soames planted Scarlet American Oaks (*Quercus coccinea* 'Splendens'), Tupelo Gum (*Nyssa sylvatica*) and Japanese maples (*Acer palmatum*) at the top end of the Ten-Foot Pond, along the north bank of which he also introduced deciduous cypresses (*Taxodium distichum*). North of the Middle Lake he concentrated large conifers, which included wellingtonia and Noble Fir. East of the Upper Woman's Way Pond there were Tree amelanchiers and more nyssas and Japanese maples, again for autumn colour.

Arthur Soames, who introduced rhododendrons to the garden

Rhododendron 'Loderi King George'

The twisted branches and vibrant autumn foliage of a Japanese maple (*Acer palmatum*)

Blue autumn gentians in beds first planted by Arthur Soames

The First Lake in October

Picea breweriana ('Brewer's Weeping Spruce') in May, when new needles are being formed

The south-west section of the garden was left as more open and wild heathland, apart from the long winding beds of autumn gentians (*Gentiana sino-ornata*), originally laid out flanking a grass path that ran from the Cascade Bridge along the north bank of the Lower Woman's Way Pond. (After the Second World War the gentians were moved to their present position, at the bottom of the Conifer Walk.) Relatively unchanged is the nearby Kalmia Walk, where he planted mainly deep pink-flowered varieties, crossing them himself to improve his strains. It was very largely Arthur Soames who created the garden we see today – a series of open walks around a succession of stepped lakes, amid huge clumps of rhododendrons and under high trees, with variety provided by the constantly changing contrasts of colour, scale and level.

Soames continued the tradition of opening the garden to the local people; another frequent visitor, who became a friend, was Queen Mary. Like the 3rd Earl, Soames was a middle-aged bachelor when he took on Sheffield Park, and his nephew, Captain Granville Soames, fully expected to inherit in due course. However, in 1919, at the age of 65, Soames suddenly married Agnes Peel, a granddaughter of the Victorian prime minister. He died in 1934, appropriately enough for such a devoted rosarian at the height of the rose season: floral tributes came from the National Rose Society and the Messel family, creators of another great Sussex garden, Nymans. His widow Agnes stayed on as tenant for life at Sheffield Park and helped to ensure that the garden survived the Second World War, when it was requisitioned by the War Office. It became the HQ for a Canadian Armoured Division before D-Day and was also used later as a POW camp; the remains of service crockery have been found in the woods.

The National Trust

Mrs Soames finally gave up Sheffield Park in 1949 to her nephew, who did much to restore the garden to its pre-war condition, with the help of T. H. Setford, Head Gardener at Sheffield Park for over 40 years. However, Captain Soames was obliged to sell up in 1953, when, regrettably, the house and garden were separated, the latter being acquired in 1954 by the National Trust with the encouragement of the RHS, and a bequest from Dr F. B. Penfold, local authority grants and money raised by a public appeal.

Since 1954 the National Trust has renewed much of the decaying original planting and dredged thousands of tons of mud from the lakes. Gardens are living things, which must change to survive, and so in the 1970s the Trust began to redevelop existing plantings under the watchful eye of Graham Stuart Thomas, its Gardens Adviser. In 1977 the Queen's Walk was created by Archie Skinner, the Head Gardener, in celebration of the Queen's Silver Jubilee. The Stream Garden was started the following year in a boggy area to the west of the Gentian Walk. The Great Storm of 1987 sadly denuded the famous lakeside plantations and the important shelter belts, but, with the vigour noted by the 1st Earl of Sheffield over 150 years ago, the garden is gradually recovering.

Taking cuttings from a conifer for propagation

A tree-lined walk in autumn

Short Tour

Towards the neo-Gothic Sheffield Park House (not open to the public) are several autumn-foliaged trees and shrubs including maples, photinias, nyssas and fothergillas. At the head of the First Lake there is a fine specimen of Blue Cedar (*Cedrus atlantica* 'Glauca'). The banks of the First and Second Lakes are broken by rounded clumps of rhododendrons in pink, white and crimson. Past the First Bridge the main path goes through groups of deciduous and evergreen azaleas and some fine old lime trees.

After you cross the Lower Bridge built by the National Trust in 1957 to replace the then unsafe Stone Bridge, there is a view to the waterfall and the house beyond. Red-, pale pink- and white-flowered water-lilies are a feature during late summer.

Following the lakeside path and beyond a weeping form of Tupelo (*Nyssa sylvatica*) are several *Fothergilla monticola*, enkianthus and parrotia for autumn colour. A Copper Beech (*Fagus sylvatica purpurea*) dominates this area with a *Cedrus atlantica* 'Glauca'. There are many fine views across the First Lake with Silver Birch, Common Oaks and specimen conifers dominating the landscape. Near the end of this path a mature oak frames the view to the house.

(Above) White water-lilies (*Nymphaea*) in bloom

(Left) The glorious autumn foliage of *Nyssa sylvatica*

Extended Tour

The Aucklandii Walk

As you take the right fork, you can see the small specimen of *Eucalyptus gunnii* planted in 1987 to replace the 1908 planting. By the path there is a group of *Rhododendron* 'Angelo', a hybrid between *Rhododendron griffithianum* and *discolor*, which is late flowering, with fragrant white to soft pink flowers. The path leads to several large groups of pink Japanese azaleas 'Hino-Mayo'.

The Conifer Walk

This was devastated by the storm of 1987, but many young specimens propagated from the original trees have now been planted. Beyond a fine specimen of *Acer saccharinum*, two long beds of Chinese gentian (*Gentiana sino-ornata*) produce rich blue trumpet-shaped flowers during early autumn.

Rhododendron 'Angelo'

Ghent azalea 'Fanny'

Ghent azaleas: the pink flowers are 'Norma' and the yellow 'Narcissiflorum'

Seven Sisters Glade

Past Seven Sisters Glade, recently replanted after the 1987 storm, there is a grove of Tupelo Trees (*Nyssa sylvatica*). These superb autumn-coloured trees have already reached 18m (60ft) in height.

The Fourth Lake

On the bank of the Fourth Lake, or Lower Woman's Way Pond, are two fine specimens of Dawn Redwood (*Metasequoia glyptostroboides*) and Swamp Cypress (*Taxodium distichum*). Beyond are clumps of the great Brazilian *Gunnera manicata*, with leaves that can reach 1.8m (6ft) wide. In the boggy ground are Bog New Zealand Flax (*Phormium tenax*). Over to the left is *Magnolia tripetala*, also known as the Umbrella Tree, which bears handsome, large leaves.

The Fourth Lake in October

The seed head of *Acer palmatum*

The Fourth Lake photographed on the shortest day of the year

The Cascade Bridge

By the Cascade Bridge is an Italian Alder (*Alnus cordata*), amongst the red stems of *Cornus alba* 'Sibirica'. The cascade links the Third and Fourth Lakes, where there were once stepping-stones that created the 'Woman's Way'. According to the legend, a headless woman is liable to appear here, vanishing when approached.

The Queen's Walk

Turning right across the Cascade Bridge, we enter the Queen's Walk, opened in 1977 to celebrate the Queen's Silver Jubilee. At the top of the Walk is the old cricket field, part of which is now an area for wild flowers including Spotted Orchids. The path continues to two small wooden bridges which cross a natural marshy area where grow Water Forget-me-nots, Water Parsnip, Tussock Sedge, Reed Mace, willows and alders. Kingfishers, herons, wild ducks and Marsh Tits may occasionally be seen also. The path, under tall alders, brings us to the corner of Big Tree Walk and a pleasing view of the Cascade Bridge across the Third Lake. Here we can see a sweetly scented *Magnolia × thompsoniana* and a Huon Pine (*Dacrydium franklinii*) and a *Stuartia malacodendron*, whose white flowers complement their blue stamens.

The Cascade Bridge between the Third and Fourth Lakes

Playing cricket on the frozen Third Lake in January 1891

The Big Tree Walk

This takes its name from the fine specimens of the North American *Sequoiadendron giganteum* which survived the 1987 storm. Beside the Walk is a number of summer-flowering azaleas, including *Rhododendron viscosum.* Beyond are further groups of *Rhododendron* 'Angelo' associated with various forms of *Rhododendron* 'Loderi' with its fragrant white to soft pink flowers during May. The somewhat unusual avenue of palms (*Trachycarpus fortunei*) form a striking effect in the surrounding informal woodland area. The main path goes past Common Oak and beech underplanted with hardy hybrid rhododendrons. Towards the First Lake there is a particularly fine specimen of the rare *Pinus montezumae*, a native of Mexico planted in 1910. On the house side of the main path two fine pollarded Sweet Chestnuts could be the remnants of a seventeenth-century avenue.

One of the old pollarded Sweet Chestnuts

Acer palmatum underplanted with Pampas Grass

The base of a *Sequoiadendron giganteum* 'Wellingtonia'